INTRODUCTION

Being a drummer calls for a great deal of physical *stamina* and *strength*, which is why I wrote this book of *speed* and *endurance* exercises. However, these exercises should be practiced with *smoothness* in mind, rather than speed. Speed will come gradually, *if* you practice every day.

It's very important for you to be relaxed and comfortable while you're playing these exercises. Work on them one page at a time. Don't push yourself; play up to your top comfortable speed. After playing a page, stop for a few minutes and then return to the same page. You'll notice how much easier it will feel.

My sticking notation is very important . . . you'll find notation for single and double stroke rolls, and paradiddles (which are a combination of singles and doubles). The sticking can get tricky, but as you become familiar with it, it will feel more natural *AND* it will strengthen both hands.

After you've mastered the sticking, and become comfortably acquainted with the exercises, you'll only have to go through this book once a day to feel your hands improve!

These exercises should serve you well, *and* will keep your hands in great shape.

Nick Ceroli

ABOUT THE AUTHOR

Nick Ceroli, born in Niles, Ohio, attended the Cincinnati Conservatory of Music for one and a half years, and then went on the road with Ralph Marterie.

After a two year stint traveling with Ray Anthony, he moved to Los Angeles in 1960, where he played with all the local bands, from Stan Kenton's to Les Brown's.

In the prime role of studio musician, he's worked with greats Peter Matz, Allyn Ferguson and Carmine Coppola and can be heard with Ray Brown and Dudley Moore in the score of Moore's movie "Six Weeks."

He's performed and recorded with singers Peggy Lee, Jack Jones, Steve Lawrence and Eydie Gorme, Vicki Carr, Irene Kral, Dave Fishberg and Cleo Laine!

Ceroli's recorded with a myriad of jazz stars including Zoot Sims, Al Cohn, Bob Florence, Mundell Lowe, Jack Sheldon, Don Menza, Alan Broadbent, Pete Christlieb, Warne Marshe, Stan Kenton, Bill Berry, Richie Kamuca and Ray Brown.

In addition to all the recording, studio and performing work, Ceroli performed on the Merv Griffin Show for seven and a half years, as well as subbing on the Tonight Show. He was also on the faculty at the Dick Grove School of Music, where he taught a weekly drum class.

SPEED and ENDURANCE STUDIES

by NICK CEROLI

CONTENTS

©Copyright MCMLXXXII by Dick Grove Publications
Copyright assigned MCMLXXXV to Alfred Publishing Co., Inc.

SECTION ONE

This section initially presents warm-ups for each individual hand, and then puts the two hands together.

By stressing the accent (with the snap of your wrist), you will build strength in your hands, as well as endurance.

STAY RELAXED!

* * *

Accented Endurance Exercises-Groups of Four

Single Stroke Endurance Exercises

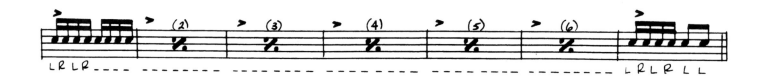

Endurance Exercises

7

RLRL _ _ _ _ _ _ _ _ _ _ _ RLRLR R R R R R   LRLR _ _ _ _ _ _ _ _ _ LRLRL L L L L L

RLRL _ _ _ _ _ _ _ _ _ _ _ _ _ _ _ _ _ _ R R R R   LRLR _ _ _ _ _ _ _ _ _ _ _ _ _ _ _ _ L L L L

RLRL _ _ _ _ _ _ _ _ _ _ _ _ _ _ _ _ _ _ R R   LRLR _ _ _ _ _ _ _ _ _ _ _ _ _ _ _ _ L L

RLRL _ R R R R LRLR L L L L RLRL RR

LRLR _ L L L L RLRL R R R R LRLR LL

Accented Endurance
Exercises-Groups of Three

More Single Stroke Endurance Exercises

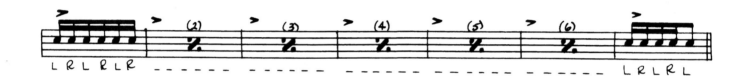

More Endurance Exercises

5. RLRLRL RLRLRL RLRL R R R R LRLRLRLRLRLRLRLR LRLR R L L L L

6. RLRLRL _ _ _ _ _ _ _ _ _ _ R R R LRLRLR _ _ _ _ _ _ _ _ _ L L L

7. RLRLRL _ _ _ _ _ _ _ _ _ R LRLRLR _ _ _ _ _ _ _ _ L

8. RLRLRL _ _ _ _ _ _ (2) _ _ _ _ _ _ (3) _ _ _ _ _ _ _ R R R

LRLRLRLRLRLR _ _ _ _ _ (2) _ _ _ _ _ (3) _ _ _ _ _ L L L

Accented Endurance
Exercises-Groups of Two

6.

R R R R — — — — — — L L — — — — — —

7.

R   R   R   R   R   R   R   R   R   R   R   R

R R   L L   L L   L L   L L   L L   L L   L L

8.

R R R R — — — — — — — — — — — —

L L L L — — — — — — — — — — — —

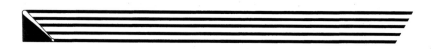

Still More Single Stroke
Endurance Exercises

17

RLRL _ _ _ _ _ _ _ _ _ _ _ _ RL R LRLR _ _ _ _ _ _ _ _ LRL

R L R L _ _ _ _ _ _ _ _ _ _ _ _

R L R LRLR _ _ _ _ _ _ _ _ _ _ _ LRL

RLRL _ _ _ _ _ _ _ _ _ _ _ _ _ _ RLR

L R L R _ _ _ _ _ _ _ _ _ _ _ _ LRL

Endurance Summary 1

Now, here are double strokes . . .
It's very important for you to make each stroke sound the same,
so that this:

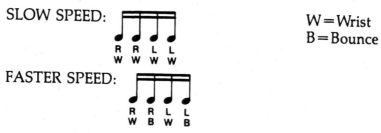

will sound the same as this:

When your speed increases, you can bounce the second stroke of
each double, but when you play at slower speeds, you should use
your wrists for each stroke:

SLOW SPEED:

FASTER SPEED:

W = Wrist
B = Bounce

Remember, *smoothness* before *speed*.

Double Strokes

3.

R R L L R R L L R R L L R R   L L R R L L R R L L R R L L

(REVERSE STICKING ON REPEAT)

4.

R R L L R R L L R R L L R R L L   R R R R R R R R
L L R R L L R R L L R R L L R R   L L L L L L L L

5.

R R L L R R L L R R L L R R L L   R R L L R R R R R R
L L R R L L R R L L R R L L R R   L L R R L L L L L L

6.

R R L L R R L L R R L L R R L L   R R L L R R L L R R R R
L L R R L L R R L L R R L L R R   L L R R L L R R L L L L

7.

R R L L — R R
L L R R — L L

8.

R R L L — R R L
L L R R — L L R

9.

R R L L —
L L R R —

More Double Strokes

RRLL RL RRLL RL RRLLRRLL RL RLRR LLRRLRL LLRRLR LLRRLLRRLRLL

RRLL _ _ _ _ _ _ _ RL RRLL _ _ _ RR LLRR _ _ _ _ _ _ _ _ LR LLRR _ _ _ _ LL RRLL

RRLLRL RRLL RL RRLL _ _ _ _ _ _ RR LLRRLRLLRRLR LLRR _ _ _ _ _ _ LL

RRLLRLRL RRLL RRLLRR LLRRLLRR LLRRLRLLRR _ _ _ _ _ _ _ _ _ LL RRLL

RRLL - R L RRLL RR   LLRR - - - - - - - - - - - - - - - - - - - L R LLRR LL

R L RRLL RL RRLL   RRLL RRLLRR LLRR   L R LLRR LR LLRR   LLRRLL RRLLRRLL

RRLL - - - - RL RRLL   - - - - - - - - - RR LLRR   - - - - LR LLRR LL   RRLL - - - - - - - - - - -

R L RRLL - - - - - - - - - - - - - RL RRLL RR   LLRRLLRRLR LLRR   LLRR LL RRLL RRLL

RRLL RRLL R L RRLL   RRLL R R LLRR LLRR   L R LLRR LLRR L L   RRLL RR LLRR LL

SECTION TWO

Before going on to the paradiddle section, practice single paradiddles for a while to warm-up:

Start slowly and gradually build to your top, comfortable speed. Hold that top speed as long as you can; keep in mind that you don't want to tighten up.

If you feel that you're getting tight, gradually slow down to your starting speed.

Watch for the accents in this paradiddle section and in the double paradiddle pages that follow.

* * *

Paradiddles

RLRRLR LRLLRL RLRRLRLL RLRRLR LRLLRL RLRRLR LRLL RLRRLRLLRL

RLRRLRLR LRLL RLRRLR LRLLRLRR LRLLRL RLRRLRLL RLRRLRLL RL RLRL

RLRRLRLL RLRRLRLL RLRRLR LRLLRL RLRRLRLL RLRRLRLL RLRRLRLLRL

RLRRLRLLRLRR LRLL RLRRLR LRLLRLRR LRLLRL RLRR LRLLRL RLRRLRLL

RLRRLRLLRL RLRR LRLLRLRR LRLLRL RLRRLRLLRL RLRRLRLL

RLRRLRLLRLRR LRLL RLRR LRLLRL RLRRLR LRLL RLRRLRLL RLRRLRLL

RLRRLRLL RRLRLL RLRRLL RLRRLRLL RRLRLL RLRRLL RLRRLRLLRL

Sixteenth Note Triplets

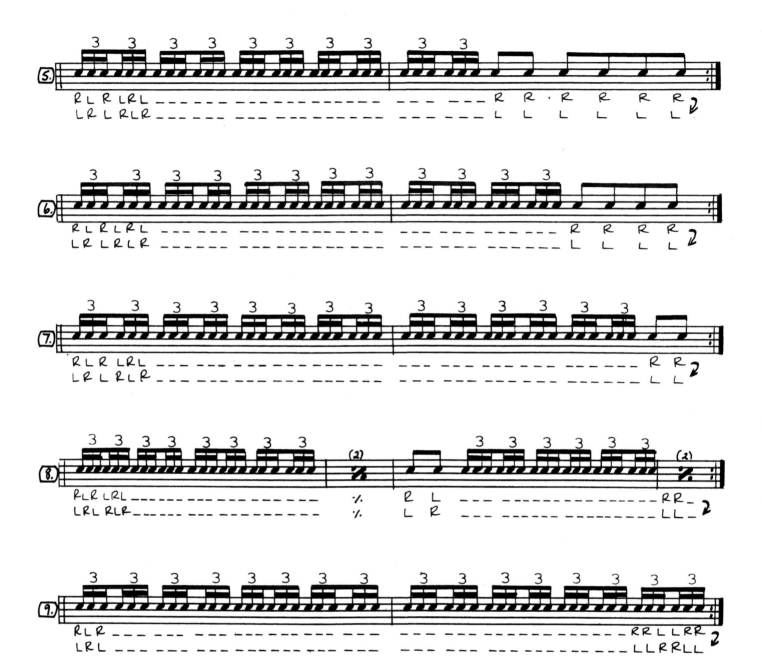

Still More Sixteenth Note Triplets

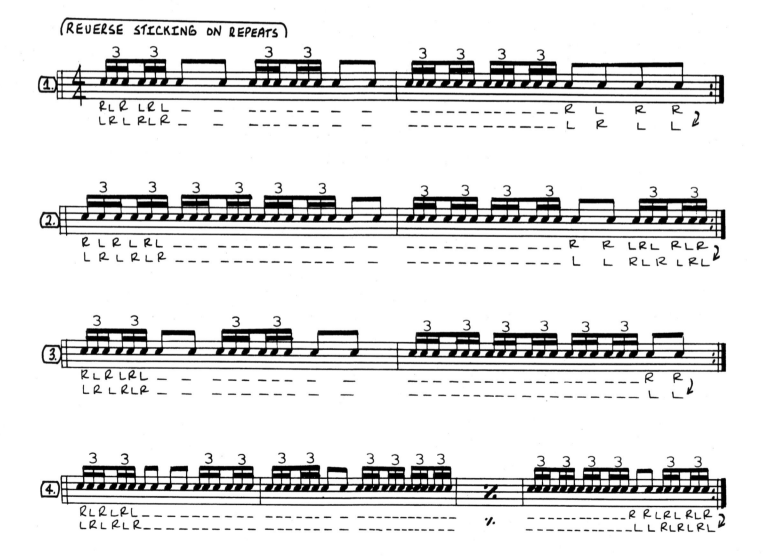

Single Stroke/Double Strokes

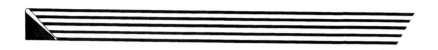

(DOUBLE STROKES)

5. RR LL RR L L L   L L L L L L   LL RR LL R R R   R R R R R R

6. RR LL RR LL RRLL   R R R R R R   LL RR LL RR LL RR   L L L L L L

7. RR LL RR LL RR LL   RR LL RR L L L   LL RR LL RR LL RR   LL RR LL R R R

8. RR LL RR LL RRLL — L L L
   LL RR LL RRLLRR — R R R R

9. RLRLRL RLRLRL   RR LL RR LL RRLL   RLR LRL RLRLRL   RR LL RR LL RRLL

Double Paradiddles

(SUMMARY)

5.

R L R L R L R L RL R L RL RL R L R L R R L R L R L L R L R L R L R L R L R L R L R L R R L R L R L L

6.

R R L L RR LL RR LL RL RL RR LRL R LL RLRL RL RL RL RL RL RL RR LRLRLL

7.

R L R L R L RR LL RR L R L R L R LL RR LL RLRL RL RR LL RR L R L R L R LL RR LL

8.

R L R L R L R L R L R R L R L R L R L R L R L L RL RL RL RL RL RL R R LRL RL RL RL RL RL L

9.

R R L L RR L R L R L L RL RL RR LL RR LL R L R L R R LL RR LL RR LL RR L RL R L L

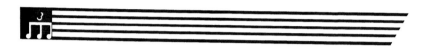

Still More Sixteenth Note Triplets

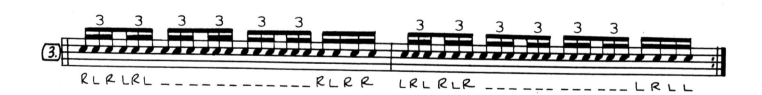

More Sixteenth Note Triplets
. . . and Paradiddles

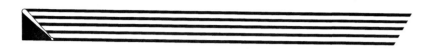

Fast Double Strokes

RRLLRRL R L R LLRRLL R L RL R L R L RRLLRRL R L R LLRRLL

RRLLRRL R L R LLRRLL RLRL RRLLRRLLRRLL R L R L RLRL

RRLLRRLLRRLL _ _ _ _ _ _ _ _ _ _ _ _ _ _ _ LR LR LLRRLL RLRL

RRLLRRLLRRLL R L RR LLRRLL RRLLRRLRLL RRLLRRLLRRLL

RLRL RRLLRRL R L R LLRRLL RRLLRRLLRRLL RLRRLRLL

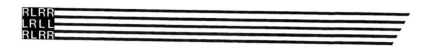

Fast Double Paradiddles

5.

R L R L R R L R L R L R L R L L R L R L R L R L R L R R L R L R L R L R L L

6.

R L R L R R L R L R L R L R L L R L R L R L R R L R L R L R L L R L R L R L R L

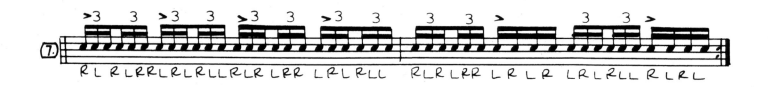

7.

R L R L R R L R L R L L R L R L R R L R L R L L R L R L R R L R L R L R L R L L R L R L

8.

R L R L R R L R L R L L R L R R L R L R L L R L R L R R L R L L R L R L R R L R L R L L

9.

R L R L R L R L R R L R L R L R L R L L R L R L R R L R L R L L R L R R L R L L

Up until now you have only had to deal with occasional accents.
From here on, accents become more *syncopated* and plentiful.
Be sure to play them correctly.

Once again, start slowly and strive for smoothness, Don't get
anxious. Stay relaxed!

* * *

Simple Accents

4. R L R R L R L L R L R R L R L R   L L R L R R L R L L R L R R L R
L R L L R L R R L R L L R L R L   R R L R L L R L R R L R L L R L

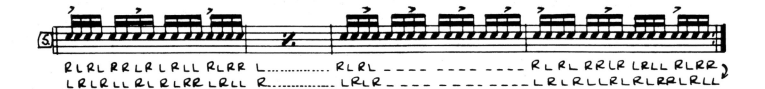

5. R L R L R R L R L R L R L L R L R R L   R L R L   R L R L R R L R L R L L R L R R
L R L R L L R L R L R R L R L L R   L R L R   L R L R L L R L R L R R L R L L

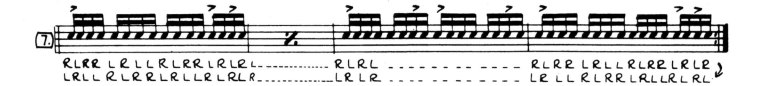

6. R L R L   R L R R
L R L R   L R L L

7. R L R R L R L L R L R R L R L R   R L R L   R L R R L R L L R L R R L R L R
L R L L R L R R L R L L R L R L R   L R L R   L R L L R L R R L R L L R L R L

8. R L R L R L R R L R L R L R L L L   R L R R L R L R L L R L R L R R
L R L R L R L L R L R L R L R R   L R L L R L R L R R L R L R L L

9. R L R L R R L R L R L R L L R L R L   R R L R L R L L R L R L R R L R
L R L R L L R L R L R R L R L R   L L R L R L R R L R L R L L L

SECTION THREE

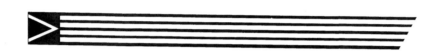

Syncopated Accents

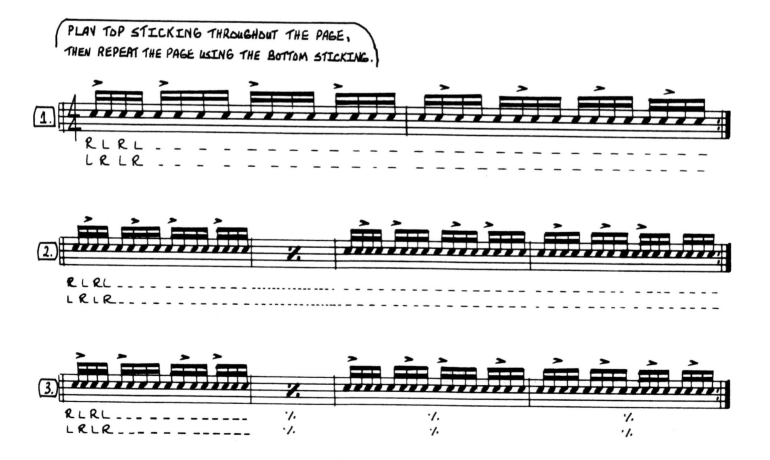

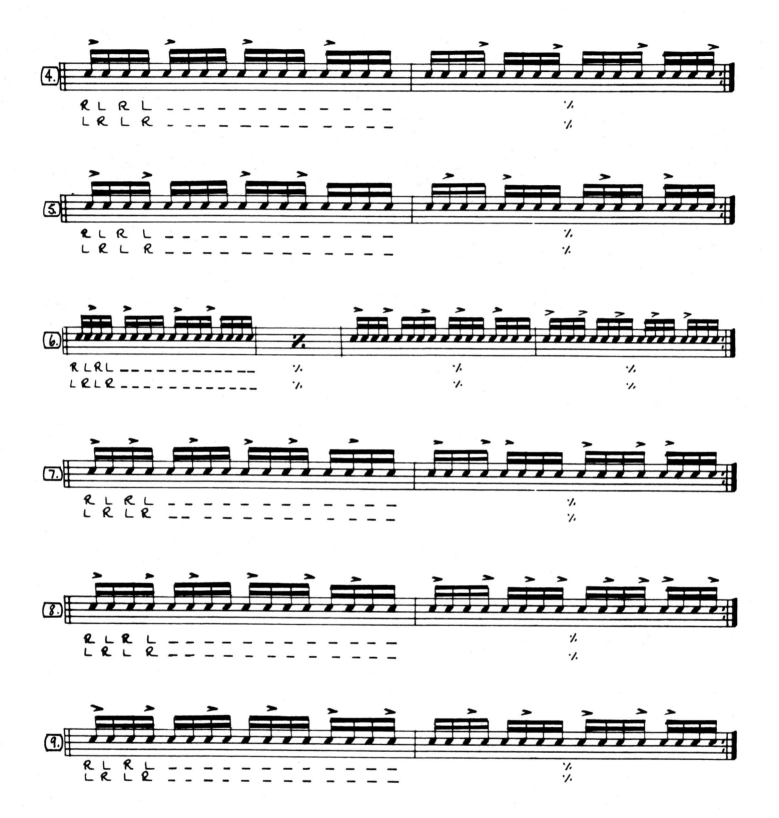

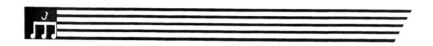

Accented Sixteenth Note Triplets

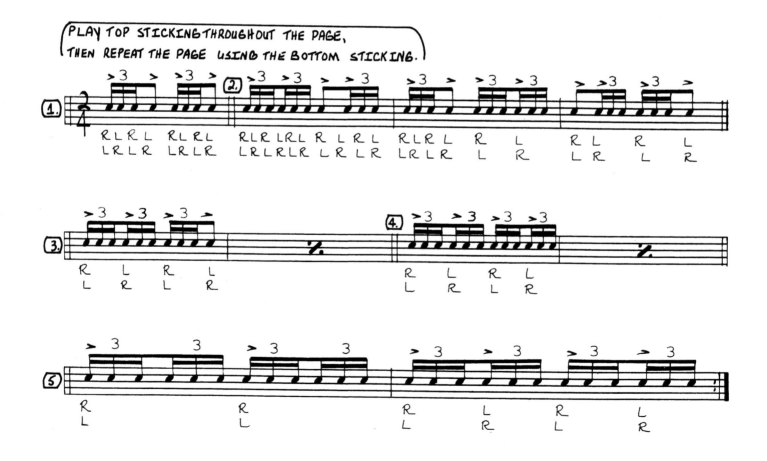

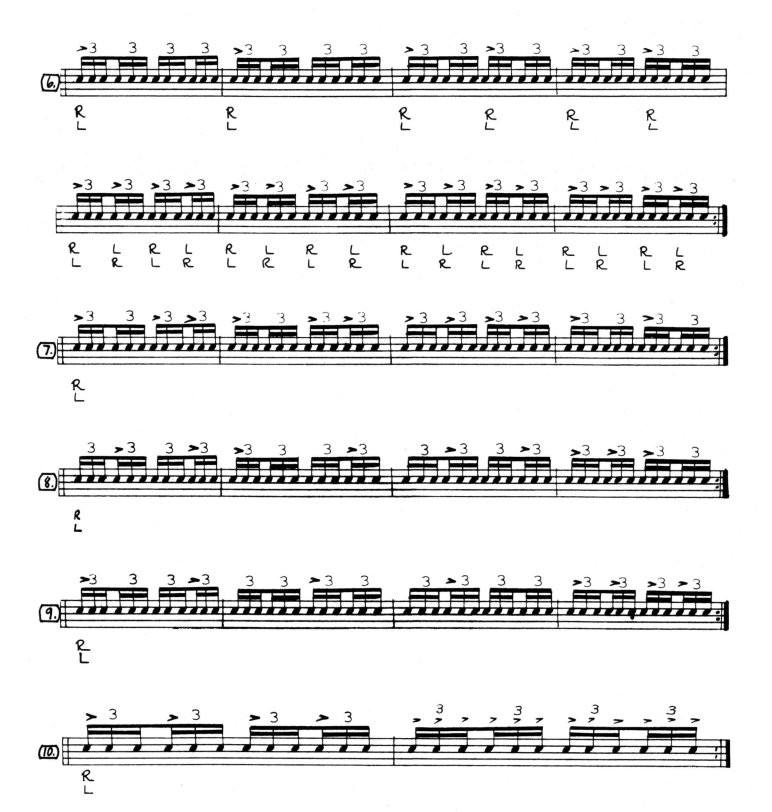

Even More Sixteenth Note Triplets

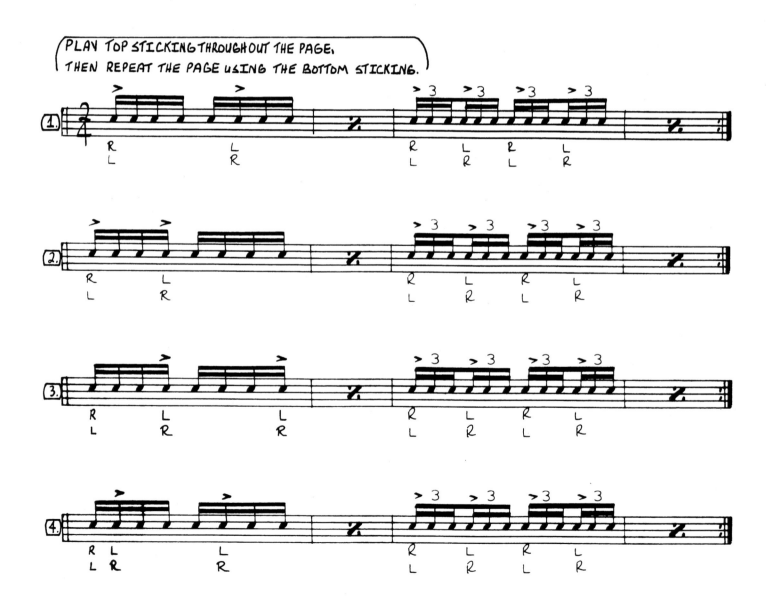

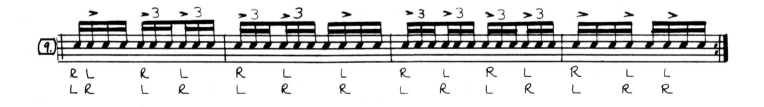

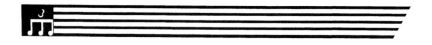

The Last Group of Sixteenth Note Triplets

Thirty-Second Notes / Single Strokes

(REVERSE STICKINGS ON REPEATS)

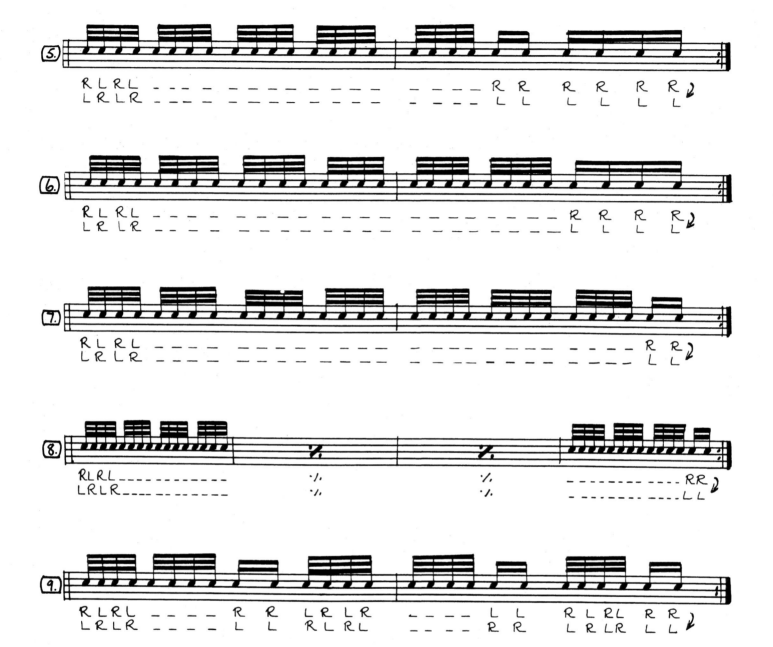

Double Strokes

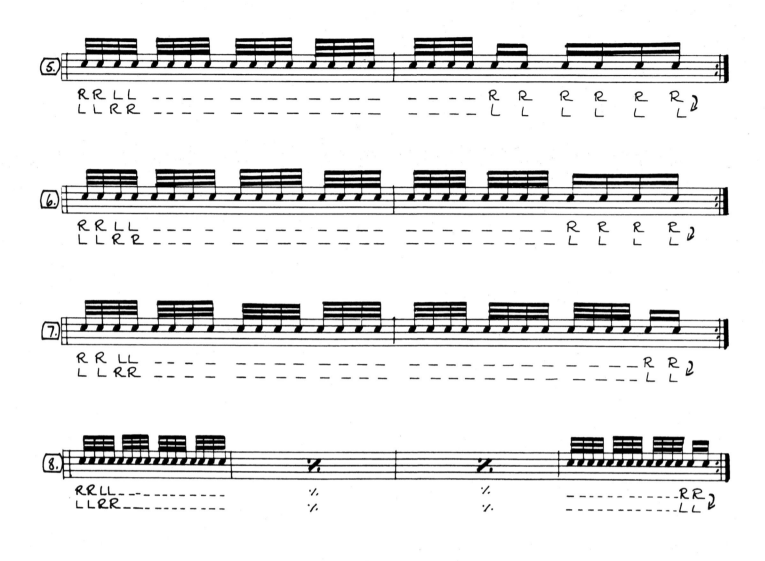

56

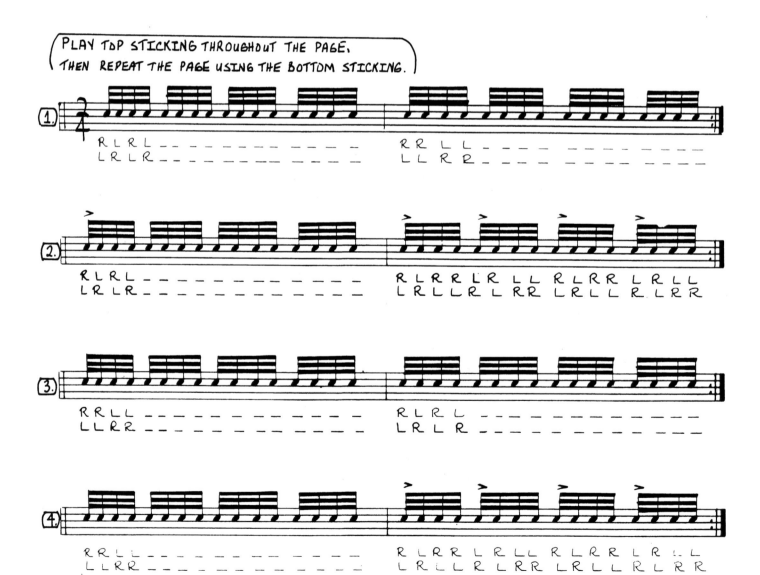

PLAY TOP STICKING THROUGHOUT THE PAGE.
THEN REPEAT THE PAGE USING THE BOTTOM STICKING.

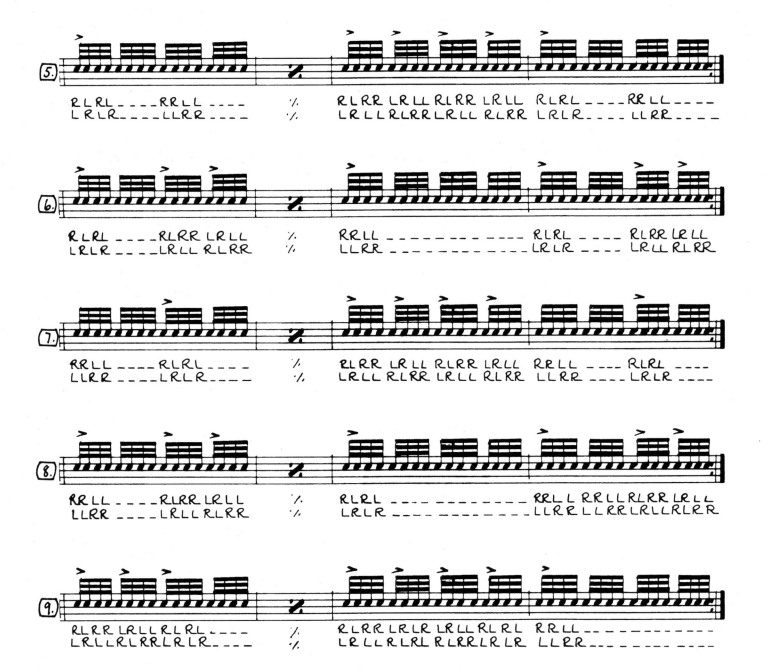